CAMBRIDGE LIBRARY COLLECTION

Books of enduring scholarly value

Perspectives from the Royal Asiatic Society

A long-standing European fascination with Asia, from the Middle East to China and Japan, came more sharply into focus during the early modern period, as voyages of exploration gave rise to commercial enterprises such as the East India companies, and their attendant colonial activities. This series is a collaborative venture between the Cambridge Library Collection and the Royal Asiatic Society of Great Britain and Ireland, founded in 1823. The series reissues works from the Royal Asiatic Society's extensive library of rare books and sponsored publications that shed light on eighteenth- and nineteenth-century European responses to the cultures of the Middle East and Asia. The selection covers Asian languages, literature, religions, philosophy, historiography, law, mathematics and science, as studied and translated by Europeans and presented for Western readers.

Two Anglo-Indian Cookery Books

A product of Britain's long political and commercial involvement in India, Anglo-Indian cuisine has since become firmly embedded in British culinary life: curries, kedgeree and chutneys have taken their place on the nation's tables. These two fascinating texts on Anglo-Indian cookery were written for the instruction of the wives of returning expatriates. Sandford Arnot's collection of recipes, which he translated from Persian and Hindustani, was first published in 1831. Arnot (*fl.* 1840) was, at the time, working at the London Oriental Institution, a college established in 1805 to teach Indian languages to civil servants. Henrietta Hervey (1850–1932) first published *Anglo-Indian Cookery at Home* in 1895. It distils her knowledge of the subject gained through twenty-three years spent living in India as the wife of a colonial officer. It is full of practical advice – from methods of preparation to the utensils required – as well as an array of colourful recipes.

T0352312

Cambridge University Press has long been a pioneer in the reissuing of out-of-print titles from its own backlist, producing digital reprints of books that are still sought after by scholars and students but could not be reprinted economically using traditional technology. The Cambridge Library Collection extends this activity to a wider range of books which are still of importance to researchers and professionals, either for the source material they contain, or as landmarks in the history of their academic discipline.

Drawing from the world-renowned collections in the Cambridge University Library and other partner libraries, and guided by the advice of experts in each subject area, Cambridge University Press is using state-of-the-art scanning machines in its own Printing House to capture the content of each book selected for inclusion. The files are processed to give a consistently clear, crisp image, and the books finished to the high quality standard for which the Press is recognised around the world. The latest print-on-demand technology ensures that the books will remain available indefinitely, and that orders for single or multiple copies can quickly be supplied.

The Cambridge Library Collection brings back to life books of enduring scholarly value (including out-of-copyright works originally issued by other publishers) across a wide range of disciplines in the humanities and social sciences and in science and technology.

Two Anglo-Indian Cookery Books

SANDFORD ARNOT
HENRIETTA A. HERVEY

CAMBRIDGE
UNIVERSITY PRESS

CAMBRIDGE UNIVERSITY PRESS

Cambridge, New York, Melbourne, Madrid, Cape Town,
Singapore, São Paolo, Delhi, Mexico City

Published in the United States of America by Cambridge University Press, New York

www.cambridge.org
Information on this title: www.cambridge.org/9781108055635

© in this compilation Cambridge University Press 2013

This edition first published 1831 and 1895
This digitally printed version 2013

ISBN 978-1-108-05563-5 Paperback

INDIAN COOKERY,

AS

PRACTISED AND DESCRIBED

BY THE

NATIVES OF THE EAST.

———

TRANSLATED

BY

SANDFORD ARNOT,

ONE OF THE CONDUCTORS OF THE LONDON ORIENTAL INSTITUTION.

3 I

TRANSLATOR'S PREFACE.

———◇———

FROM our political and commercial relation with India, it is well known that a very considerable number of individuals and families in this country have, from a long residence in the East, acquired a strong predilection for Indian modes of life. Many of these, peculiar to the climate, and sometimes termed "the luxuries of the East," must necessarily be left behind in quitting it. Some, however, are capable of being transplanted: and as a great moral philosopher has observed that it is the aggregate of small enjoyments which forms the bulk of the sum of human happiness, whatever contributes to so important a result cannot be considered as altogether unworthy of notice. Therefore, since amid the vast change of circumstances which retired Indians must experience on their return home, the difference in the practice of the

culinary art is not the least considerable, both
as regards comfort and as regards health, the
Oriental Translation Committee have thought it
worth while to include the following short treatise among the miscellaneous pieces published
under their auspices.

The Translator hopes it will prove an acceptable present to many old Indians, who,
however much they may have relished the
pleasures of the table while in the East, most
probably, like himself, never took the trouble
to enquire how their favourite dainties were
produced ; leaving this entirely to the assiduity
and skill of the useful artist known by the
name of the *Bábarchí* (or báwarchí) and other
native servants who penetrated the mysteries
of the *Bábarchí khánah*. Had we lived in the
days when, as history informs us, female edu-
cation comprehended a thorough knowledge of
cookery and comfits, " preserves " and " con-
serves," our fair countrywomen in India might
have explored this field of discovery. But in
these degenerate modern days, it is to be feared
that few of them in that sultry climate ever
encountered the heat and smoke of the Bábarchí

khánah, or even discussed its delicate processes with the swarthy operator. Consequently, on their return to Europe they consider it no imputation on their housewifery to be quite unable to give instructions how to perform the simple every-day operation of boiling rice or cooking a curry. To the study of Indian written lore they are in general still less addicted : therefore it is to be hoped that they will kindly excuse this attempt to supply in some small degree what is now felt to be a desideratum. The example may induce others to make further discoveries in a field hitherto so little investigated.

The treatise, of which the following is a translation, presented to the Royal Asiatic Society, by C. Elliot, Esq., bears internal marks of being written by a native of the Bengal side of India, and is composed in the Persian language, with a slight admixture of Hindustani phrases. As it has no pretensions to literary elegance, the translation has assumed none. The weights introduced are calculated by the Calcutta Bazar *maund*, and reduced as nearly as practicable to our own avoirdupois weight, omitting

fractions.   A table of the relative value of the
weights used, according to the best authorities,
is subjoined.

		lb.	oz.	drs.	Drops.	
A Ser	=	2	0	13	13·648	Avoirdupois
A Pā'o (¼)	=	0	8	3	7·888	do.
A Chattank	=	0	2	0	14·208	do.
A Māsha	=	0	0	0	10·5129	do.
A Dām	=	0	0	0	2·6282	do.
A Ratti	=	0	0	0	1·3141	do.

London Oriental Institution,
2, *South Crescent, Bedford Square,*
June 13, 1831.

CONTENTS.

——◆——

AUTHOR'S PREFACE.

———◇———

He who facilitates.

In the name of God, the peculiarly merciful and
gracious.

Treatise in Explanation of Delicious Foods and Meats.

LET it be known to the whole community who are
intelligent, and who have a taste for learning and the
arts, that whereas the excellent disposition of the
gallant Captain Paxon (may God perfect his nature),
a gentleman of high dignity, an appreciator of learning, skilled in the rules of India, qualified to esti-
mate the sciences of Arabia and Persia, of high re-
pute and full of intelligence, is much inclined to-
wards the meats of India and its delightful dishes;
therefore, with the approbation of that gentleman, some
kinds of fine dishes are herein described in a brief
manner.

INDIAN COOKERY.

No. 1.

YAKHNÍ PULÁ'O.

Ingredients.

Take common Rice, ½ ser (1 lb. avoirdupois).

Meat gravy, 4 sers (8 lb.)

A piece of kid (or lamb), 1½ ser (3 lb.)

Butter, 3 pá'o (1½ lb.)

Milk, ½ ser (1 lb.)

Cream, ½ ser (1 lb.)

Coagulated milk (boiled), 1 pá'o (½ lb.)

Almonds, ½ ser (1 lb.)

Cardamums, 2 dáms (5 drops).

Cloves, 6 máshas (4 drops).

Cinnamon, 6 máshas (4 drops).

Salt, 1 chittank (2 oz.)

Lemon, ½ pá'o (¼ lb.)

Rosewater, 2 dáms (4 drops).

First, let all the pieces of meat be washed seven or
eight times, until the water used come off pure, and they

be quite clean. After that put four pounds of good water into the pot, and throw into it the pieces already mentioned, and let them boil; and, while boiling, remove the scum that may appear on the water. When, in the boiling, two pounds of the water only remain, take it down from the fire-place, strain it through a cloth, and put this gravy-juice into the butter. After that put into it half the weight of the cardamums, and replace it on the fire-place. Afterwards take it off, and select the heavy pieces carefully from the others; put them into the pot in which the gravy is, and having passed it upon the trivet, let it boil. When half the soup remains, put into it lime-juice and salt, and take it down from the fire-place. Then, having peeled and ground the almonds, put the almonds, cream, and coagulated milk altogether; strain them through a fine cloth, and throw them amongst the soup and pieces (of meat, &c.). Having steeped the rice in water for two hours before this, now remove the water, and put fresh water into the pot corresponding to it, and make it boil. When it is somewhat ready, strain it through a cloth, and put it into the pot containing the gravy and ingredients (pieces); and, having closed the mouth of the pot with flour, put it on the fire. When the steam rises from the pot, take it down, and, having put hot charcoal round it, stew it; and after about twenty-four minutes open its mouth and serve it up.

No. 2.

FRIED FOWL OF MUHAMMED SHAH.

Take Rice, ½ ser (1 lb. avoir.)

 Meat gravy, 1 ser (2 lb.)

 A fowl.

 Butter, ½ ser (1 lb.)

 Cream, ¼ ser (½ lb.)

 Milk, ¼ ser (½ lb.)

 Boiled milk, ¼ ser (½ lb.)

 Almonds, ¼ ser (½ lb.)

 Aniseed (or wild onion), 2 masha.

 Salt, 1 chittank (2 oz.)

 Cardamums, 4 masha, (2½ drachms).

 Cloves, 2 masha (1¼ drachms).

 Cinnamon, 2 masha (1¼ ditto).

 Raw ginger, 1 chittank (2 oz.)

 Lime, 1 chittank (2 oz.)

 Dry coriander, 4 masha (2½ drs.)

First clean the fowl, and pierce it with the point of the knife; then having ground half the weight of the ginger and salt together, rub it into the fowl; put the butter into the pot, and place it on the fire; and having mixed the curdled milk with the fowl, throw it into the pot with the butter, and dress it with a slow fire. When it is well browned, throw in a quarter of a pound of water, and take it off the fire. The cream and the milk and the ground almonds, strain through a cloth, and put

them into the pot: add lemon. Then having taken
about two pounds of flesh, washed and cleaned, and put
it into a pot of proper size, boil it. When four pounds of
water are reduced to two, take it off, strain and boil the
rice in the meat gravy and sprinkle it with salt: then
take it off, and having strained it, throw the rice into the
pot containing the fowl; and having put in anniseed,
cinnamon, cloves, and cardamums, close the mouth of the
pot with flour, and replace it on the trivet and cook it
with a gentle fire. When the steam rises, having taken it
down, put it on a charcoal fire and place some of the
coals round it, and after twenty-four minutes, open the
mouth of the pot and serve it up.

No. 3.

A LIGHT PULÁ'O.

Take Rice, $\frac{1}{4}$ ser (1 lb.)

Meat gravy, 1 ser (2 lbs.)

Butter, $\frac{1}{2}$ ser (1 lb.)

Kid or lamb, $\frac{1}{2}$ ser (1 lb.)

Cream, $\frac{1}{4}$ ser ($\frac{1}{2}$ lb.)

Almonds, $\frac{1}{4}$ ser ($\frac{1}{2}$ lb.)

Boiled milk, $\frac{1}{4}$ ser ($\frac{1}{2}$ lb.)

Milk, $\frac{1}{4}$ ser ($\frac{1}{2}$ lb.)

Salt, 1 chittank (2 oz.)

Dry coriander, 2 dams (5 drops).

Cinnamon, 2 masha ($1\frac{1}{4}$ drachms).

Cardamums, 2 masha (1¼ drachm).

Cloves, 2 ditto (1¼ ditto).

Raw ginger, 1 chittank (2 oz.)

Lemon, 1 chittank (2 oz.)

Aniseed, 2 masha, (1¼ drs).

The mode of forming it is this: First remove all the bones from the flesh, and having made it into slices, let it be half scored through with the knife ; grind half the quantity of cardamums and of the cloves, and all the coriander, and half the salt ; add the boiled milk, and having mixed them into the slices and put them into the butter, fry them. When it becomes brown add ⅛ of water ; take it off, and after this having mixed together the ground almonds, the cream and milk, and strained them, throw them into the kettle : add lemon. Then having taken up the meat gravy, and thrown the rice into it, give it a half boil. Throw in the remainder of the salt, and having strained the rice through a cloth, throw it into the butter and the collops (or slices). Then having put in the cloves, cardamums, and cinnamon, close the mouth with flour. Then pass it on the fire, and when the steam rises take it off the trivet, and put it on the coals, then stew it for twenty-four minutes; put a little of the coals round it, and when it has stewed suffi-ciently, eat it.

No. 4.

KHICHARY.

Take Dāl, or mung (a kind of pease), ¼ ser, (½ lb. avoir.)

 Common rice, ¼ ser, (½ lb.)

 Butter, ½ ser, (1 lb.)

 Milk, ¼ ser, (½ lb.)

 Salt, ½ chittank, (1 oz.)

 Whole cardamums, 2 masha, (1¼ drs.)

 Cloves, ½ masha, (5 drops).

There are two modes of preparing this dish. It may be cooked in an earthen pot or a copper kettle. First put two pounds of water into the pot and place it on the fire. When the water becomes hot put in the pease, having first washed them in three or four waters, and when they are ready cooked, throw in your butter, cloves, and whole cardamums ; and, if you have a nice (luxurious) taste, put milk into the *khichary*. After this, close the mouth of it with flour, and place it on a coal fire, and stew it.

If you wish to make *khichary* of pease or pulse (cytisus cajan, cicer lens, or ervum lens, or hirsutum), the mode is that which has been described ; and if shelled pease be agreeable, let them be so, and make the same composition. If it be the kind of pulse called cytisus cajan of which you wish to make *khichary*, first boil the pease, then mix in the rice in the manner above mentioned. When it is cooked, stew it over hot ashes, and then serve it up.

––––––

No. 5.

A SMALL FRIED KHICHARY.

Take common Rice, $\frac{1}{4}$ ser ($\frac{1}{2}$ lb. avoir.)

　　Dal Mung (pease) $\frac{1}{4}$ ser ($\frac{1}{2}$ lb.)

　　Butter, $\frac{1}{2}$ ser (1 lb.)

　　Onions, $\frac{1}{2}$ chittank (1 oz.)

　　Cloves, 2 masha ($1\frac{1}{4}$ drachms).

　　Cardamums, 2 masha, ($1\frac{1}{4}$ ditto).

　　Black Pepper, 2 ditto ($1\frac{1}{4}$ ditto).

　　Anniseed, 2 ditto ($1\frac{1}{4}$ ditto).

　　Salt, $\frac{1}{2}$ chittank (1 oz.)

This is the composition: Having put the butter into the kettle, and sliced the onions and put them into the butter, place it on the fire-place, and having washed the khichary (qu. pease?) put it in along with the onions: having also put the said ingredients quite entire and unground into the butter, fry the khichary. When it becomes brown put in half a ser (one pound) of water, and when the khichary becomes tender and nice to the taste, take it off the trivet, close up the mouth with flour, and replace it on a coal fire. After a while (*ghari*, twenty-four minutes), when it has been stewed and become ready, open it and serve it up.

No. 6.

COMPOSITION FOR MAKING KORMAH.

Take Meat, ½ ser (1 lb.)

    Butter, ¼ ditto (½ lb.)

    Salt, ½ chittank (1 oz.)

    Boiled milk, ¼ ser (½ lb.)

    Cream, 1 chittank (2 oz.)

    Ginger, ½ ditto (1 oz.)

    Lemon, ½ ditto (1 oz.)

    Dry Coriander, ½ *dam* (1⅓ drops).

    Cloves, 1 masha (10½ drops).

    Cardamums, 1 ditto (10½ ditto).

    Black Pepper, 4 ditto (2½ drachms).

    Saffron, 1 masha (10½ drops).

Wash the flesh and mix it with the salt and essence of ginger; then take the boiled (coagulated) milk, and having pressed out the water through a strainer, and the cream strained through a cloth, mix the two latter ingredients with the meat, and fry the onions (cut coat by coat) with the butter. When it becomes brown, throw the meat into the butter, and the cloves and whole cardamums; and having roasted and peeled the coriander put it in also. When the meat becomes brown with frying, put in ¼ ser (½ lb.) of water, and cook it till the flesh becomes tender. Having then put in the black pepper, lemon-juice and saffron, take it off the trivet, and put it on a coal fire and stew it. Then serve it up for eating.

No. 7.

DOPIYAZAH.

Take Meat, $\frac{1}{2}$ ser (1 lb. avoir.)

    Butter, $\frac{1}{4}$ ser ($\frac{1}{2}$ lb.)

    Salt, $\frac{1}{2}$ chittank (1 oz.)

    Ginger, $\frac{1}{2}$ ditto (1 oz.)

    Onion, 1 ditto (2 oz.)

    Boiled Milk, $\frac{1}{4}$ ser ($\frac{1}{2}$ lb.)

    Cream, 1 chittank (2 oz.)

    Lemon, $\frac{1}{2}$ ditto (1 oz.)

    Dry Coriander, $\frac{1}{2}$ dam ($1\frac{1}{3}$ drops).

    Clove, 1 masha (10 drops).

    Cardamums, 1 ditto (10 drops).

    Black Pepper, 4 ditto ($2\frac{1}{2}$ drams).

    Turmeric (Haldi), 4 ditto ($2\frac{1}{2}$ ditto).

    One clove of Garlick.

Having cleaned and washed the meat, mix with it the salt, essence of ginger, and boiled milk and cream, strained through a cloth. Cut the onions coat by coat, and fry them in oil of butter.* Having pounded the turmeric and garlick, and strained them through a cloth, and mixed them with the meat, throw the same into the butter. Put in the cloves and whole cardamums, and the coriander, fried and peeled. When the flesh

---

* Or melted butter, probably the *ghee* or melted butter of India, so well known there in commerce and cookery, but which is not once mentioned, at least by its Indian name, in this treatise.

has been fried, put in half a ser of water.   Then try the
flesh with the hand.   When it has become nice and tender, put in the black pepper and lemon.   Take it off the
trivet, and stew it over charcoal (or hot ashes), and after
that serve it up.

No. 8.

VEGETABLE CURRIES.

Preparation of Meat with every kind of Vegetable.

If the vegetable be *Arwí* (a species of Aram, the root
of which is used in food), or *Tará'í* (a kind of cucumber), put four ounces into one pound of meat, with
spices, boiled milk &c., the same as mentioned in the
Dopiyázah ; but leave out the cloves, cardamums, and
prepared almonds.   First having removed the skin of
the Aram or the cucumber, and washed them, and fried
the flesh in butter, put it into a proper kettle and fry
the Aram or cucumber in that butter.   Then having
mixed the flesh and vegetables, and put in half a ser of
water, cook it till the flesh become tender: then put in
black pepper and lemon, and if you please saffron : however, it is very good without it.

If the vegetable be turnip, first remove the skin of the
turnip, and cut it with the point of the knife ; put in
salt and squeeze it until the water flow out.   Then dry
it with the strainer, and fry it in the said butter ; and

having put in the flesh add a quarter of a seer of water. When the flesh has become tender put in the pepper, lemon, and saffron, and place it on the fire. When cooked take it off the trivet, and stew it over a charcoal fire or hot ashes; and in this manner you may cook any vegetable with flesh.*

No. 9.

PURSINDAH SÍKHÍ.

Take Flesh, ½ ser (1 lb.)

Butter, ⅛ ser (4 oz.)

Salt, ½ chittank (1 oz.)

Onion, ½ ditto (1 oz.)

Cream, 1 ditto (2 oz.)

Coagulated milk, ¼ ser (½ lb.)

Juice of 1 lemon (límú kághazí).

Coriander, 1 dam (2½ drops).

Pepper 4 masha (2½ drachms).

Saffron, 4 ratti (5 drops).

Cloves, 1 masha (10½ ditto).

Cardamums, 1 ditto (10½ ditto).

Raw ginger, 1 chittank, (2 oz.)

First having prepared the pieces of flesh, score them half through, mix the salt and lemon juice; then mix in the coriander (roasted and peeled), the cloves and cardamums, and the pepper (ground down): then the coagu-

* See Note at the end.

lated milk (entirely freed from its watery part) : then the onion cut down coat by coat, and browned in oil. Mix the butter in the flesh with the onion. After this, put the slices of flesh on the spit, and rub on them the ground saffron, and the cream strained through a cloth and mixed together, and fry it on a coal fire, having first made the coals red hot; and when it is well browned serve it up.

No. 10.

FRIED FOWL.

Having taken a fowl well cleaned and washed, and pierced it with the point of the knife, mix it with ½ a chittank (1 oz.) of raw ginger, ½ pao (4 oz.) of coriander peeled and ground, and cloves and cardamums and ground pepper, and coagulated milk quite freed of the water, and cream strained through a cloth ; and having taken half a chittank (1 oz.) of onion cut down very small, fry it in butter, mix it with the fowl, and in this manner fry it.

No. 11.

KABÁB-I KHATÁE.

A Tartar or Chinese Roast.

Take Flesh, ½ a ser (1 lb.)

Butter, ¼ ditto (½ lb.)

Salt, $\frac{1}{4}$ chittank (1 oz.)

Coagulated milk, $\frac{1}{4}$ ser ($\frac{1}{2}$ lb.)

Cream, 1 chittank, (2 oz.)

Onion, 1 chittank (2 oz.)

Coriander, 1 dam (2$\frac{1}{2}$ drops).

Two lemons.

Black pepper, 4 masha (2$\frac{1}{2}$ drachms).

Saffron, 4 ratti (5 drops).

One hen's egg.

Flour of vetches (roasted), 1 dam (2$\frac{1}{2}$ drops).

Cloves, 1 masha (10$\frac{1}{2}$ drops).

Cardamums, 1 masha (10$\frac{1}{2}$ drops).

Raw ginger, 1 chittank (2 oz.)

Having minced the meat and put it into a mortar and pounded it, mix it with salt and essence of ginger: and then having pounded the coriander roasted and peeled, the black pepper, cloves, cardamums, and half the weight of the onions bruised, and having ground the saffron, put the whole into the hash; also the coagulated milk quite freed from the water, and flour of vetches roasted; also put the white and yolk of the egg and the cream into the hash. Throw the butter into a fish pan, and having formed the hash or mince into cakes, put them into the fish pan, and well brown them over a coal fire. When they become brown, add lemon juice, and then having taken them out of the frying pan, serve them up whenever you please.

No. 12.

FISH ROASTED ON A SPIT.

Take the flesh of Fish, $\frac{1}{2}$ ser (1 lb.)

  Butter, $\frac{1}{2}$ pao (4 oz.)

  Raw ginger, $\frac{1}{2}$ chittank (1 oz.)

  Onion, ditto (1 oz.)

  Coagulated milk, $\frac{1}{4}$ ser ($\frac{1}{2}$ lb.)

  Cream, 1 chittank (2 oz.)

  Coriander, 2 falus.

  Flour of vetches or pulse, $\frac{1}{2}$ chittank (1 oz.)

  Pepper, 4 masha ($2\frac{1}{2}$ drams).

  Clove, 1 masha ($10\frac{1}{2}$ drops).

  Cardamums, 1 masha ($10\frac{1}{2}$ drops).

  One lemon.

  Salt, 2 dams (5 drops).

First having formed the flesh into pieces fit for roasting, and pierced them with the point of the knife, wash them well with the pease-flour. After that put on them the salt, and essence of ginger and coriander peeled and ground, and pounded pepper. And having fried the onions, cut down very small, in butter, mix them with the roasts along with the butter: add the lemon-juice, cloves, and cardamums ground, and the coagulated milk freed of water, and the cream strained. Then having put the pieces on the spit, rub on them the spices (or seasoning ingredients) that remain, and fry them on the fire.

No. 13.

PRESERVE OF MANGOES.

Take unripe Mangoes, $\frac{1}{2}$ ser (1 lb.)

    Loaf sugar, 1 ser (2 lb.)

    Lemon, $\frac{1}{4}$ ser ($\frac{1}{2}$ lb.)

    Quick lime, 1 dam ($2\frac{1}{2}$ drops.)

Having peeled the mangoes and cut them in two pieces and pierced them with the point of the knife, get half a ser ready, and throw it into the water. Then, having mixed the quick lime with water in another vessel, throw the mangoes into that lime and water. Then, having taken them out and put them into pure water, boil them : when they become soft take them out of the water and dry them. And having thrown the sugar into water and formed a syrup, and removed the scum and turbidness, try it between two fingers; and when it has attained somewhat of a glutinous consistency, put three pao (1 lb. 8 oz.) of the syrup in a proper-sized vessel, and having thrown in three-quarters [pao?], let it boil. Then take it off the fire. Let the mangoes remain in the syrup for two watches or a whole day. Afterwards again boil three pao (1 lb. 8 oz.) of the syrup, and, having taken the mangoes out of the first syrup, throw them into the second.

No. 14.

KHÁGÍNA (Omelette).

Take ten hen's eggs.

Melted butter, ½ pao (4 oz.)
Flour of roasted pease, 1 chittank (2 oz.)
Salt, ¾ chittank (1 oz.)
Pepper, 4 mashas (2½ drams.)
Coriander, roasted and peeled, 1 dam (2½ drops.)
Cloves, 1 masha (10¼ drops.)
Cardamums, 1 masha (10½ drops.)
Onions, 1 chittank (2 oz.)
Coagulated milk, ½ pao (4 oz.)

Having broken the eggs, and ground together the flour of pease and pepper, and sliced down the raw onion, and pounded the coriander, cloves, and cardamums, throw them in and mix them: then, having removed the water from the curdled milk, mingle them well together; and having thrown them along with the milk into a frying-pan, heat it over a coal fire, and throw the whole of the eggs into the melted butter. After when one side is browned, having cut it in pieces with the knife, take it off and use it.

No. 15.

TALÁWÍ TARKÁRÍ.

Take Butter, ½ ser (1 lb.)
Flour of pease, ½ ser (1 lb.)
Coagulated milk, ¼ ser (½ lb.)

Salt, 4 dams (10½ drops.)

Cloves, 1 masha (10½ drops.)

Cardamums, 1 masha (10½ drops.)

Coriander, 4 masha (2½ drams.)

Pepper, 4 masha (2½ drams.)

Cucumber, 1 ser (2 lb.)

First, having removed the skin of the cucumber and cut it into long slices, and put in half the weight of salt, keep it aside. Mix the flour of pease and coagulated milk together, and having pounded the cloves and cardamums and salt and coriander and pepper altogether, mix them with the pease-flour, and having put the butter into the frying-pan, place it over a coal fire. And having dipped the slices of cucumber, one by one, into the pease-flour, throw them into the butter, and brown them on both sides. After that, having taken them off, use them. By the same preparation, every vegetable whatever, such as pumpkin (or pompion) and love-apple (the Indian brinjal), &c., may be fried and eaten.

No. 16.

FRIED FISH.

Take Fish, ½ ser (1 lb.)

Butter, ½ pao (4 oz.)

Pease-flour, ¼ ser (½ lb.)

Coagulated milk, ¼ ser (½ lb.)

Cloves, 1 masha (10½ drops.)

Coriander, 4 masha (2½ drachms.)

Pepper, 4 mash (2½ drachms.)

Salt, ½ chittank (1 oz.)

First having cut the fish into pieces, and strained the coagulated milk and the pease flour, and ground down the rest of the ingredients, mix them with the fish; and having put the butter into the frying pan, place it on the fire. When it becomes hot, having thrown the pieces of fish besprinkled or besmeared with the spices into the butter, fry them. When they become brown on both sides, take them out of the butter, and eat them.

No. 17.

PURI.

Take Flour, ½ ser (1 lb.)

Salt, 1 chittank (2 oz.)

Butter, ½ ser (1 lb.)

Flesh, ½ ditto (1 lb.)

Coagulated milk, ½ pao (4 oz.)

Milk, ¼ ser (½ lb.)

Cloves, 1 masha (10½ drops).

Cardamums, 1 masha (10½ drops).

Onions, 1 dam (2½ drops).

Ginger, 1 ditto (2½ drops).

Coriander, ½ dam (1⅓ drops).

Pepper, 2 masha (1¼ drachms)

Having hashed the meat, wash it well, and mix with it half the quantity of the salt, and the spices ground and pounded down, and the coagulated milk, and having put one chittank of butter into the vessel, place it on the fire and fry the flesh. When it becomes brown, add a little water. When it becomes tender put it on a plate : and having mixed two dams of butter in the flour and thrown in the milk, form a paste, but let it not be soft, rather somewhat firm. After this, having made it into balls, form it into cakes on a table with the roller. Then place one below and one above with the hash just between them, and close the edges, and having thrown the butter into the frying pan, and put the cakes into it, brown both sides of them.

No. 18.

HALWAE BADAM.

(Comfit of Almonds).

Take Almonds, 1 ser (2 lb.)

Loaf sugar, $\frac{1}{4}$ ser ($\frac{1}{2}$ lb.)

Butter, 4 dams (10$\frac{1}{2}$ drops).

Flour, $\frac{1}{4}$ ser ($\frac{1}{2}$ lb.)

Having broken the almonds, and taken the kernels and boiled them in hot water, peel them. Then having mixed them in flour, fry them. When the almonds and flour become browned, having separated them from the flour and cleaned them well in a (sieve), throw them into

a mortar and pound them.   When they become like
flour, having put the sugar into half a pao of water, prepare a syrup, and remove the impurities of it; and
having taken the syrup in the two fingers, try it.   When
it has attained a degree of consistency, throw into it the
pounded almonds and the butter, and mix them.   If you
wish it to be perfumed put in a little rose-water.

No. 19.

HALWAE ZARDAK.

Take Almonds, $\frac{1}{4}$ ser ($\frac{1}{2}$ lb.)

　　　Loaf sugar, $\frac{1}{2}$ ser (1 lb.)

　　　Carrot, 6 ser (12 lb.)

Having peeled the carrot, boil it: when it becomes
very soft, put it in a filter, and squeeze out the water,
and having weighed whatever remains in the filter, take
$\frac{1}{2}$ a ser (1 lb.) and having made a syrup of the sugar
put it on the fire, and clear away the scum and impurities.   When it acquires something of a consistency, throw
the said $\frac{1}{2}$ ser (1 lb.) of carrot in the syrup.   Throw in
(the butter?) also.   And when it attains a consistency,
put into it the almonds, each cut into four pieces or
whole.   And if you wish it scented put in some saffron
and rose-water.

No. 20.

TAMARIND PRESERVE.

Take raw Tamarind, ¼ ser (½ lb.)

Loaf sugar, ½ ser (1 lb.)

Lemon, 1 chittank (2 oz.)

Having removed the skin of the raw tamarind and extracted the seeds, take ¼ ser and make a syrup of the sugar in half a pao (4 oz.) of water, and remove its impurities. When it settles, throw in the tamarind and cook it, and when it acquires a consistency add lemon-juice, and take it off the fire and cool it ; and keep it, and take it out and use it when required.

No. 21.

MANGO PICKLE.

Into a hundred mangoes deprived of the skin, put 1 pao (8 oz.) of salt, and keep them in a vessel. And having taken moist or raw ginger, cut down fine, mint also, and a little garlick likewise if it be agreeable to your taste, and having cut down a little of the mango piece meal, mixed with salt corresponding to it, put it into a dish, and having cleaned and dried the mangoes well through a filter so that no moisture may remain, then split them in the middle so that they may not come apart, and fill the centre of them with the said spices: then tie a raw thread over them, and throw them into

mint or vinegar, with some salt over them.   When after
three or four days the pickle becomes soft and mild, use
it when required.

RICE MILK.

Take Milk, 1 ser (2 lb. avoir.)
    Rice, $\frac{1}{2}$ poa (4 oz.)
    Loaf sugar, $\frac{1}{4}$ ser ($\frac{1}{2}$ lb.)

Having softened the rice in water, and put the milk
into the pot, place it on the fire and boil it.   After
twenty-four minutes take the rice out of the water, dry
it with the strainer and throw it into the milk and boil
it.   When the rice has become somewhat soft put in the
sugar, and mix it with the ladle.   Then put it into a
fresh earthen vessel, cool it, and add rose-water, for the
sake of the perfume, should it please your taste.

JAGHRAT.

(*Milk thickened by boiling.*)

Having put 4 sers (8 lb.) of pure milk into a pot,
boil it.   When 2 sers remain, cool it ; but let some of
the milk remain warm.   Then having taken a fresh
earthen vessel washed clean, heat it a little on the fire ;
then having put the said milk in it, and dissolved in it

three dams (9 drops) of runnet, (or sour milk used to coagulate fresh milk,) mix it with that boiled milk which has been put aside. Having put it immediately into a vessel, close the mouth of it carefully and cover it up, and in the cold season protect it still more, and place some warm ashes under it, till it coagulates. If you like sweet curds, mix with the milk $\frac{1}{4}$ pao (2 oz.) of sugar in boiling it.

———

No. 24.

LEMON PICKLE.

Take Lemon, 10 sers (20 lb. avoir.)
   Salt, 2 half sers (2 pounds.)
   Ginger, 2 half sers (2 pounds.)

Take half the quantity of the lemons (i. e. five sers) cut into four parts, and put the salt and ginger into them; press out the juice of the other half (5 sers) and throw it in, and should there be a deficiency of juice, throw in that of another ser besides. Place the whole in the sun for forty days successively, and take it in at night.

3 N

No. 25.

CHATNEE.

Having removed the skins and seeds of ten sers (20lbs.) of mangoes, and broken them down very small, not removing the juice that may come out, take

Ginger, ½ pao (4 oz. 7 ds. avoir.)

Salt, according to taste.

Cloves, 1 dam (2½ drops.)

Black pepper, 1 ditto (2½ ditto.)

Nigella Indica, 1 ditto (2½ ditto.)

Red pepper (Cayenne) 1 ditto (2½ ditto.)

Dry coriander seeds (the kernels of them) 6 mashas (4 drams.)

Mace, 1 masha (10½ drops.)

Dry spear mint, 1 dam (2½ drops.)

Cinnamon, 1 dam (2½ drops.)

Having pounded and bruised these ingredients, and put in also ¼ ser (½lb.) of the juice of mint, keep it in the sun for the space of fifteen days. When the juice of the mint may have been dried up, put some mint juice into the *chatnee*, then keep it and use it when you please.

N O T E.

P. 21.

It may be found useful to compare this Receipt for making vegetable Curries with the ordinary receipt for making Curry followed in England, which is so simple that any one may reduce it to practice.

Receipt for making Indian Curry.

Take fowl, neck of mutton, rabbit, or veal, about 1lb.; cut it off the bones into small pieces; mix with it three or four onions cut small; add three or four potatoes with pepper and salt; also, if you please, a boiling apple minced down small. Dissolve the curry-powder (about two table-spoonfuls of it) in half a pint of water. Put $\frac{1}{4}$lb. of lard or butter into the stewpan; and when that is melted, put in all the above ingredients together and strew them over a slow fire, carefully stirring them all the time until the vegetables be entirely dissolved. When the curry is about half done put in two or three eggs, first boiled hard and chopped small. When the meat is sufficiently done, serve it up as hot as possible. Fowl or mutton curries are best.

Receipt for Boiling Rice.

Take half a pound of rice; clean it in salt and water; put it into two quarts of boiling water, and boil it briskly for about twenty minutes; then strain it in a cullender, and shake it into a dish, but do not touch it with your fingers or a spoon. In India it is generally allowed to steam for about five minutes over the fire after the water has been poured off, in order to render it somewhat dry.

Printed by
J. L. COX, GREAT QUEEN STREET,
Lincoln's-Inn Fields.

ANGLO-INDIAN COOKERY
AT HOME:

A SHORT TREATISE FOR RETURNED EXILES.

BY

THE WIFE OF A RETIRED INDIAN OFFICER.

LONDON:
HORACE COX,
"The Queen" Office, Windsor House, Bream's Buildings, E.C.

1895.

LONDON:
PRINTED BY HORACE COX, WINDSOR HOUSE, BREAM'S BUILDINGS.

PREFACE.

INASMUCH as the demand for books on Anglo-Indian cookery and housekeeping still exists, in spite of the many excellent works already published on these subjects, I am induced to compile this little volume with a hope that it may prove acceptable to those Anglo-Indian ladies who are not too proud to supplement their experience with mine. It is my endeavour, therefore, to give in these pages the result of knowledge gained during twenty-three years of married life in India, and which, I sincerely trust, may be of service to those who, having finally quitted the East, may still hanker, now and again, after the fleshpots of the land of their exile. As I have resided in various parts of India, I submit I am in a position to strike a fair average, whereby my wrinkles and recipes may be acceptable to those whose lots may erewhile have been cast anywhere from Peshawur to Cape Comorin; from Kurrachee to Calcutta. My aim being to supply a cookery book for "Old Indians" in England, I have not, as a rule, given vernacular terms, weights, or quantities, endeavouring to adapt my instructions to the conditions ruling here, which are somewhat different to those obtaining out yonder.

I could give many more recipes on all culinary subjects

and yet be within my profession—*i.e.*, the furnishing of a guide to Anglo-Indian Cookery in England—but the many difficulties to contend with in producing all but the plainer styles of dishes are so obvious, that I feel sure my fellow Anglo-Indians and the general Public will pardon the small dimensions of the book wherewith I seek to gain their favour.

HENRIETTA A. HERVEY,

The Wife of a Retired Indian Officer.

Hammersmith, W.,
November, 1894.

ANGLO-INDIAN COOKERY AT HOME.

SOME HINTS.

PROVIDE yourself with a set of agate or enamel ware utensils, with, preferably, flat-handled lids. I brought home my "Dekchies"—tinned just previous to embarking at Bombay—but, in due course, they required the attentions of the "Kalai Man," and I looked for him and his grimy assistant in vain. I was told to try Whiteley; but his prices for "Kalying" I found to be so prohibitive, that my "Dekchies" have been consigned to the kitchen cupboard as useless.

I strongly advise the purchase of a mincing or sausage machine, to be firmly fixed to the dresser. English kitchens, as a rule, are boarded, and in close proximity to the dwelling-rooms. More, they are resonant, and the average English servant, be she cook or "general," is *not* light-handed. Chopping, therefore, is inconvenient; the noise is not mellowed by distance, as is the case in India. So, if there be any objection to a machine, provide a corner of the dresser or kitchen table with a small stone slab. By placing a thick board on the slab, and chopping thereon, the sound will be minimised. By keeping the kitchen door shut as much as possible, opening the

B

window when feasible, that objectionable feature of English domestic life, to wit, the "smell of dinner," will be appreciably ameliorated.

To those of us who have a weakness for the soft fresh bread of the Indian "Roti Walli," the dryasdust London article is an infliction. I find the only way to keep bread from drying up altogether is to deposit it in an earthen pan and cover the mouth with a clean damp cloth of several folds.

Though butter, lard, and dripping *are* substitutes for "ghee," still, for Indian cookery there is nothing like this last. I intend giving a recipe for the making of "ghee," and I very strongly advise its adoption when making up anything from this little book.

The English servant, I find, *is* open to instruction. Ours, a raw country Essex girl, has learnt to boil rice as well as any old "Thunnikurchi" or cook-boy out there, and I am hopeful of being able to entrust her with curries, &c., at no very distant date. Patience is a virtue and—everything.

SOUPS.

Mock Turtle Soup.—Take a calf's head, and remove the skin by soaking it for a couple of hours in cold water. When thoroughly cleansed, put the head into a large saucepan, pour on cold water sufficient to cover, and place on a moderate fire till it boils. Now take off the lid, and remove the scum. Let the soup simmer gently for seven hours, or until the bone and meat separate, when strain off through a clean towel, and set aside till quite cold. The grease will now have come to the surface, and must be carefully removed. Replace the soup on a slow fire for five minutes, again set aside to cool, add a little sweet herb, a shred of celery, the peel of half a lemon, the whisked whites and crushed shells of two eggs. Pour the mixture from one saucepan to another, which greatly helps the process of clearing, replace on fire, allowing the whole to boil; then let it settle for a few minutes, after which strain through another clean towel. Before serving, add sufficient " browning," salt to taste, and, at the last moment, a glass of good sherry. Have ready in the tureen some thin slices of the soup-meat and tongue, and on which pour the boiling soup.

Mulligatawny Soup.—A tablespoonful of " ghee," or butter, and an onion sliced. Put both into a saucepan,

with a few curry leaves (if procurable). Fry till brown.
Add a large tablespoonful of curry paste or powder, and
fry. Take a fowl or chicken, already jointed, and the
back cut in three portions : add this to the above with a
large teacup of cold water. Cover the saucepan, and boil
slowly till the meat is tender. Now add tamarind to
taste (or vinegar), and half a cocoanut, ground to a paste,
or the extracted milk. Boil all together till the grease is
seen to rise to the surface, and, just before it comes to
table squeeze in a little lime or lemon juice.

Pea-Fowl Mulligatawny Soup.—Having cleaned and
jointed the fowl, boil in about three quarts of water with
some black peppercorns and a small quantity of mixed
spices. Continue boiling for three hours, removing the
scum frequently. Now strain and keep aside. Fry
some of the fowl meat with sliced onion, to a deep brown
with butter ; throw it into the liquor ; replace on the fire,
and boil gently for some minutes. Now put in a tablespoonful of curry-powder or paste, and let the whole boil
gently till the meat is tender.

Dholl or Split Pea Soup.—Soak about a pint of them
in water for some hours ; then boil till they are sufficiently
soft to be easily mashed. Put the mass into some stock
with a little lean bacon or ham bone, and a piece of
celery. Boil for half-an-hour. Accompany the soup
with some bread, cut in dice, and fried crisp.

Plain Rice Soup.—Thoroughly wash a handful of rice
(Bengal preferably), parboil and dry it. Having already
made some good gravy soup, well seasoned, add your rice,

and give the whole a boil till the rice is thoroughly done. The making of the gravy soup is sufficiently well understood in this country to need any instructions from me.

Pepper Water Soup.—This is such a favourite with most old Indians, especially those who have lived in the Madras Presidency, that I must be excused from dwelling at some length on the subject.

No. 1. PLAIN PEPPER WATER SOUP.—Get together the following ingredients : Coriander, cummin, and mustard seed, mixed, one dessertspoonful. Dried capsicums or chillies, from one to six. Saffron powder, half a dessertspoonful. Garlic, three cloves. Tamarind, two ounces. Barring the last two, dry (in the oven) and thoroughly pound the others; then put the whole in a saucepan with a quart of cold water, mix well, cover close, and boil for forty minutes. After allowing the liquor to settle, strain it through a clean rough towel. Into another vessel put a dessertspoonful of "ghee" or butter, in which fry half an onion to a dark brown ; over this pour your soup, previously strained, and give it a boil up. It can be drunk like tea from a cup or eaten like curry or mulligatawny with boiled rice. An excellent remedy for a "sick headache."

No. II. DHALL, OR RED PULSE PEPPER WATER SOUP.—In two pints of water, boil a large cupful of the grain till sufficiently soft, and strain it. Into the same water put the following, *well ground*: A small piece ot saffron or turmeric, one or two chillies or capsicums, a few cloves of garlic, and a teaspoonful of each of the following, pepper, mustard, cummin seeds, also a tablespoonful of either tamarind water or vinegar. Boil for twenty minutes. In another pan, fry half an onion in "ghee" or butter well brown, pour in your pepper water, and give the whole another boil. To be eaten in the same way as the last.

No. III. Dhall, or Red Pulse Pepper Water Soup.—Preferably in an iron pan, fry an ounce of the pulse and an ounce of black pepper with a dessertspoonful of "ghee" or butter; having done which. grind or pound the mixture to a paste. Add two tablespoonsful of tamarind water and two teacups of water, and as it boils add a teaspoonful each of cummin, fenugreek, and mustard seed, previously fried in "ghee" or butter. Eat in the same way.

No. IV. Prawn Powder Pepper Water Soup.— Make your soup as in No. I.; add two dessertspoonsfuls of prawn powder and a little lime or lemon juice; give it one boil and serve. To be eaten as the others.

FISH.

Fried Fish.—The Indian method is somewhat different to the ordinary English one, so I give it. Having first washed your fish, dip it in a "pigment" of saffron powder and water, which will have the effect of giving the fish a yellow colour. Powder it over with a little salt, and then dab it lightly with a dry cloth. Having beaten up an egg, and got ready some breadcrumbs, dip the fish into the egg and then into the breadcrumbs. Fry till light brown, in plenty of "ghee," lard, or dripping.

Fish Molee.—This is best made of fish that has previously been fried. Put it in a saucepan with one small sliced onion (of the size ordinarily procurable here), a couple of ounces of sliced green ginger, three or four cut green chillies or capsicums, and a little saffron or turmeric powder. Stir in the milk of half a cocoanut and the juice of a lemon. Keep over a slow fire for ten minutes. This makes a favourite breakfast dish, essentially Indian. It can be eaten like curry with boiled rice or with bread.

Tamarind Fish.—Take four or five pounds of good fish (salmon or cod are the best for the purpose in this country), scale, clean, and cut into inch-thick slices. Rub each piece well with salt, and let the whole stand for a day, or even longer. Then dry with a cloth, and place on a clean dish exposed to the air for several hours, turning the fish occasionally. Take a pound of dried tamarind, plunge it into boiling vinegar (about two quarts), and having mashed it well, extract the juice, which should be of the consistency of pulp. Take three ounces of dried red chillies, and two ounces of garlic ; grind both with vinegar into a paste. Add a tablespoonful of saffron or turmeric powder and mix all into the tamarind juice. Then souse your fish, piece by piece, in the mixture, and put into wide-mouthed bottles, pouring over the residue of the mixture. To be eaten, fried in " ghee " or butter, either as a relish with curry or by itself, with boiled rice or bread and butter.

Salted Fish Roe. Home Made.—This is another Indian delicacy one misses so much in England. The roes must be quite fresh. Rub them thoroughly with common salt, and let stand for twenty-four hours. Dry them with a soft cloth, and put them in the sun or near the fire, till all the semblance of moisture has disappeared. Wrap them separately in paper, and keep in large mouth glass bottles. To eat them, fry as you would fish. They give a zest to curry and rice, or bread and butter. 'Ware cats if you dry your roes in the sun!

Salt Fish Pie.—I give this recipe with some diffidence, inasmuch as the peculiar piquant flavour of good Indian cured fish, and which alone renders this pie so attractive, is wanting in the home production. At least, such is my humble opinion. However, I may possibly be wrong.

Having soaked your fish the previous night, boil it, remove the skin and bones, and set it aside to cool. Have ready six hard-boiled eggs, three raw onions, and some boiled potatoes, all sliced thin. Now commence to build up your pie dish with successive layers of potato, onion, fish, and egg, introducing a little pepper (no salt) between the layers. When the dish is full pour in two tablespoonfuls of anchovy and any other sauce, mixed; put in a lump of butter, lard, or dripping; crown all with potato crust, paint with yolk of egg, and bake till brown.

Twice Laid.—Here is a favourite way of disposing of any fish "remainders" out yonder. Take a pound of cold boiled or fried fish; bone it, and mash it up with six or eight well-boiled potatoes. Add a dessertspoonful of salad oil, a dessertspoonful of anchovy sauce, a tablespoonful of vinegar, a pinch or two of red pepper, and the juice of half a lemon. Mix all well together, put it into a buttered pie dish, cover with beaten egg, and bake till brown.

CURRIES.

Note.—Here in England. I find Crosse and Blackwell's the nearest approach to the real article in the way of curry powder. It will be understood, therefore, that in this chapter, when curry powder is mentioned, 1 allude to that supplied by the above-named well-known firm. The concoction of curry powder, however, is greatly a matter of individual taste, both as regards flavour aud pungency; but to procure it exactly in accordance with one's own ideas of fitness, would, in this country, be a matter of much expense, if not difficulty. I brought home a small supply, made on my own recipe, but, alas! it soon ran out, and the fall back on Crosse and Blackwell's (for we are inveterate curry eaters!) is a *pis aller* at the best. Those to whom time and expense is of no consequence, I could not better advise than to procure their curry powder, paste, &c., from Messrs. Spencer and Co., or Messrs. Oakes and Co.. both of the Mount Road, Madras. The "Benighted Presidency," remember is, *par excellence*, the home of curry and rice, and where the ingredients are produced and blended to perfection. There is an *on dit* down there that when the Prince of Wales was on his Indian tour he was actuated into wishing to visit Madras solely by a desire of tasting a Madras prawn curry at our famous club. True, Bengal and Bombay have their respective especial brands, but their curry-making is poor in comparison to that of the Madrasees. On the P. and O. they ring the changes on the three Presidencies with regard to their curries, serving Madras, Bombay, and Bengal day after day in monotonous sequence; but the strangest part of it is that the curries are all made with the same powder; your own palate proves this beyond a doubt. But now to my task.

Chicken Curry.—Take a chicken or a young fowl; skin, clean, and joint it, dividing the back bone into three. Put a tablespoonful of " ghee," butter, lard, or dripping into a stewpan with one shredded onion, and fry till brown. Now add a few cloves of garlic, and a tablespoonful of curry powder; and fry all together for some minutes, taking care that the mixture does not " catch" at the bottom of the pan. Throw in your meat and fry for several minutes, stirring briskly. Next pour in a breakfastcup and a half of water with a little salt, give it a thorough stir; cover, and boil gently for fifteen minutes. Now uncover, and as soon as the gravy thickens (*i.e.*, the water has boiled away), add a teacupful of cocoanut milk, or cow's milk, and again boil for five minutes. As soon as the grease rises to the surface, pour in a tablespoonful of tamarind water, vinegar, or the juice of half a lemon. Keep on the fire for a few minutes longer, then serve.

Fresh Mutton Curry.—The neck is undeniably the best part. Cut up and wash one pound of meat, fry your onion (as above), add your garlic and curry powder, fry all well together, then put in the mutton; fry it in the mixture, and, when well amalgamated, add two breakfast-cupfuls of water and a little salt; cover, and let it simmer gently for about fifteen minutes, or until you find the meat tender and the liquid perceptibly diminished. Now add a teacupful of cocoanut or cow's milk; go on simmering till the grease appears at the surface and the gravy thickens, when add a tablespoonful of tamarind water, vinegar, or the juice of half a lemon, and serve.

Cold Meat (any kind) Curry.—Cut it up into dice, and proceed exactly as if you were dealing with fresh mutton (as above), only omitting the two breakfast cupfuls of water and its attendant fifteen minutes boil.

Ball Curry.—You will find a mincing machine handy in making this, our noisy Indian method of chopping and mincing being impracticable in this country. Any description of meat will do ; mince a pound of it. Grind to a paste the following : A piece of green ginger, a little allspice and salt, half an onion, half a garlic. Mash this paste with the mince meat and the yolk of one egg. Fashion the mixture into balls, the size of large cherries, and fry them in " ghee," butter, dripping, or lard. Your balls now being ready, take them out of the grease, which utilise by frying therein one sliced onion till brown ; then add a tablespoonful of curry powder and fry, after which pour in a teacup of cocoanut or cow's milk and give it a boil, when add the balls, cover, and allow to simmer for ten minutes. Now uncover, stirring occasionally till the gravy thickens, when add a tablespoonful of tamarind water, vinegar, or juice of half a lemon, and serve.

Malay Curry.—Called also Ceylon Curry. A delicious preparation, and an agreeable change. Chicken, mutton, or fish can be used. The following requisites are indispensable, and should be all at hand before commencing operations :— A whole cocoanut, a tablespoonful of coriander, a tablespoonful of poppy seed, an ounce of green ginger, six green chillies or capsicums, a teaspoonful of powdered saffron, one onion, a little garlic, allspice, and salt. Pound or grind the coriander and poppy seed into a paste. Mix the saffron powder with a little water. Peel and slice the green ginger and onion. Peel and bruise the garlic. Cut your meat or fish into small pieces (if chicken, joint it), put it into a saucepan; add all the above ingredients, and pour in a breakfast-cup of cocoanut milk (of course extracted from the nut aforesaid; cows' milk will *not* answer for this curry). Give the whole a stirring, put on the lid, and let it boil gently for ten minutes. Now uncover, and pour in half a cupful more of cocoanut milk, then a tablespoonful of lemon juice; and finally allow it to simmer gently for fifteen minutes. The addition of vegetable marrow or cucumber *with the meat* is a great improvement.

"Khoormah" Curry.—This is a Mahometan dish, and, if made successfully, constitutes an agreeable change from our "English" curries. Get together the following ingredients :—Two tablespoonfuls of coriander, six cloves of garlic, six *red* chillies, one onion, half an ounce of green ginger, one tablespoonful of salt. Pound or grind all these into a paste. Take two pounds of mutton, cut into small pieces, and mix with the paste till both are thoroughly amalgamated. Now mix in two tablespoonfuls of *fresh butter*, two breakfastcups of milk curds, a little allspice, and an onion thinly sliced. Put all into a saucepan, and allow to simmer gently till the liquid almost all disappears. Eat with " Chupatties " or flour cakes (which see further on).

"**Kabob**" **Curry.**—For this you require skewers. Ordinary metal knitting needles, cut to about four inches long, looped like a key head at one end and sharpened at the other, will answer admirably. To make up a dozen skewers of "Kabob" you will require as follows :— One pound of mutton from the leg, some small onions about the size of cherries, some green chillies or capsicums, a root or two of green ginger, some cloves of garlic. Cut the meat in small pieces, halve the onions, slice the green ginger and the green chillies or capsicums. Now skewer on the meat, the onion, the chillies or capsicums, the green ginger and garlic alternately; packing close from hilt to point. Put a tablespoonful of " ghee," lard, butter, or dripping into a rather large stewpan, add a tablespoonful of curry powder, and fry well. Now put in your skewers, carefully rolling them in the pan for five minutes; pour in water enough to cover the skewers, add a little salt, and boil for ten minutes. Now add a breakfast cupful of cocoanut or cows' milk, and boil gently for another ten minutes. As soon as the gravy thickens, add a tablespoonful of tamarind water, vinegar, or juice of half a lemon, and serve. Note, that by lubricating the skewers with a little grease, previous to charging, the curry is easily detachable by means of a fork; otherwise, as any old Indian knows, the consequences may be disastrous !

Fish Curry.—Soles and cod are, I think, the most suitable. Get two pounds filleted at the fishmonger's. Wash the fish and sprinkle with a little salt. Put it into a stewpan with weak tamarind water enough to cover, and let it simmer on a *slow* fire for fifteen minutes. In another vessel, in a tablespoonful of " ghee," lard, butter, or dripping, fry a sliced onion and a little garlic; to which, when brown, add a tablespoonful of curry powder; fry for two minutes, and then add the contents of the other stewpan; cover and let it simmer for twenty minutes. Now uncover, stir gingerly, and as soon as the gravy thickens, serve.

Prawn Curry.—Immerse a soup-plateful of small prawns into boiling salted water; shell, head, and tail them, put into a stewpan, and add weak tamarind water sufficient to cover; then mix in two tablespoonfuls of curry powder, and add a green chillie, a clove of garlic, a little allspice, and sliced ginger. Stir, and allow to stand for half an hour. In a second pan brown a sliced onion in the usual manner, add the contents of the other pan, and boil gently for half an hour and serve.

Crab Curry.—Boil a good sized crab, and break the meat as little as possible while taking it out of the shell. Take two tablespoonfuls of "ghee," butter, lard, or dripping, put it in a pan, and bring to a boil. Throw in a sliced onion, a few cloves of garlic, and a tablespoonful of curry powder; fry well; then add the crab meat, and continue frying for two minutes longer. Now pour in half a breakfast cupful of cocoanut or cow's milk and serve. Remember your crab is already cooked.

Dry Curry.—Cut up a pound of any meat very small, almost minced. Put it in a pan with a large tablespoonful of "ghee," butter, lard, or dripping, a clove of garlic,

a tablespoonful of curry powder, and one onion sliced.
Fry all together over a slow fire. As soon as the grease
disappears, add salt and a tablespoonful of tamarind
water, vinegar, or lemon juice, and serve.

Egg Curry.—Hard-boil some eggs; shell, cut in half,
and keep aside. Into a pan put a tablespoonful of
"ghee," butter, lard, or dripping, and a sliced onion,
some garlic, a tablespoonful of curry powder, and fry for
two minutes; then add a breakfast cupful of cocoanut or
cow's milk and a little salt. As soon as the liquid boils
away, add half a cup of tamarind water; give one boil
and pour this gravy over your previously prepared eggs,
and serve.

Tomato Curry with Prawns.—Prepare your prawns as
shewn in recipe (above) for plain prawn curry, and have
ready the following :—Six green chillies sliced, a teaspoonful of salt, one whole garlic, one sliced onion, a small
piece of green ginger sliced, and a tablespoonful of
coriander with two red chillies reduced to a paste. Put
a dozen large tomatoes in boiling water. Place in a stewpan two tablespoonfuls of "ghee," butter, lard, or
dripping; add the prawns with the salt and fry well.
Next put in the green chillies, garlic, onions, green ginger,
and coriander-chillie paste. Continue frying for some
minutes longer, then throw in the tomatoes, previously
halved, and the milk of a whole cocoanut or a breakfast-
cupful of cow's milk. Let the whole simmer over a
gentle fire till the gravy gets thick, when serve.

"Dhall," or Split Lentils Curry.—Take a breakfast-
cup of lentils and sift it free of gravel or small stones;

then partially parch it in a dry pan over a clear fire. This done, put it in a stewpan; add cold water with a little saffron; simmer gently till the grain is soft and the water has nigh boiled away. In another pan, fry one sliced onion till brown; throw in a chillie, also the boiled lentils, and fry the whole together, seasoning with salt and cayenne pepper. The curry should be of the consistency of mashed potatoes.

Cold Fowl, or "Country Captain" Curry.—Fry an onion till quite crisp in a tablespoonful of "ghee," butter, lard, or dripping. Remove the onion and place by the fire. Joint your cold fowl, pepper it well with curry powder, then fry in the same grease you used for the onion; continue this, stirring briskly, till the grease disappears. Now place the meat in a dish and scatter on your crisped onions and a little salt. Be careful to prevent the meat from burning while being fried.

c

RICE.

To Boil Plain Rice.—Take, say, a pound of Patna rice, wash well in cold water, and drain it. Have ready a somewhat large vessel of boiling water, throw in the rice, and stir occasionally. To know if done, try a grain between the finger and thumb. When sufficiently soft, add a cupful of cold water, and give a good stir ; then drain off all the water, shake the vessel, and place near the fire to strain.

Another Method.—First spread it on a table or cloth, and pick out all the stones or gravel; then wash in two or three different waters, rubbing the rice well between the hands ; add a little lemon juice, or alum powder to whiten it ; drain and throw it into a large quantity of water ; let it boil gently, and continue until it is tender, or only a small core in the centre remains ; throw it in a cullender and let it drain for a few minutes ; then return it into the saucepan and place it near the fire, so that it may steam quite dry.

"Kitcherry" Rice.—Take half a pint of "dhall," or split lentils or dry peas, and steep them in water ; to this add half a pound of clean rice, a little sliced green ginger, salt and allspice ; boil gently till the grain is tender and the water evaporates. Previously prepare six hard boiled eggs, cut in two, and some crisped onions. Heap the rice and " dhall " on a dish, and garnish with the eggs and onion. To be a success, every grain of both rice and " dhall " should be separate.

Cocoanut Rice.—Steep, say, a pound of fine rice in water for half an hour, after which drain it thoroughly. Take the milk of two cocoanuts and pour over the rice, adding cold water if necessary till the grain is fully immersed ; throw in a little saffron powder (this last to tinge the rice), cover, and allow to boil very gently. When done, and in order to steam or dry it, proceed exactly as per directions for boiling plain rice.

Mutton "Pullow" Rice.— Take a pound of fine rice and wash it well, allowing it to soak till you are ready for it. Bruise a whole garlic, an ounce of green ginger, a teaspoonful of salt, and throw all three into a large cupful of butter milk or whey; stir well and put this mixture over a couple of pounds of young mutton. Now heat a breakfast cupful of "ghee," or butter (lard and dripping won't do) in a good sized vessel, fry in it one sliced onion till brown, add the meat, and continue frying for ten minutes. Now pour in a large cup of rich milk, then your rice, with an eggspoonful of powdered allspice, and add water sufficient to immerse the rice and meat ; this last if necessary. Cover and boil gently till the rice is *nearly* done, when remove the pan from the fire, uncover, and place it by the side or on the top of the boiler or oven for half-an-hour. A little lemon juice, added on removing from off the fire, is an improvement. This dish is called " Ukhnee pullow " by the Mahometans, and is made to the greatest perfection in Hyderabad Deccan.

C 2

Fowl "Pullow" Rice.—Clean, truss, and boil a half-grown fowl. Take a pound of thinly sliced mutton and one whole onion, place in six quarts of water, and boil till reduced to one-third. Now remove from the fire, and, with a wooden spoon, mash the meat and onion *in* the broth ; strain through coarse muslin and keep the "liquor" by. Now wash half a pound of fine rice and dry it well. Melt half a pound of "ghee" or butter in a large saucepan, and in it fry a teacupful of shredded onion till crisp and brown ; take out the onion, and in the butter that remains slightly fry your previously boiled fowl. Take out the fowl, and again in the *same* butter slightly fry the rice. As soon as the butter evaporates, add your "liquor" and boil the rice in it; add a teaspoonful of allspice, a little salt, and a few slices of green ginger. When the rice is done, considerably reduce your fire, and place some red-hot embers *on* the *pan cover*. Let it be for a few minutes, when introduce the fowl, with a view to imparting a flavour of the bird. Let it stand for another five minutes, and serve, heaping the rice over the fowl, garnishing with halved hard-boiled eggs and the crisped onions.

"English" Pullow.—This is the recipe for the dish as is generally seen on Anglo-Indian tables. The same process is observed, with but little variation, throughout the empire. Wash and soak in cold water for twenty minutes a pound of Patna or other fine rice. In a large stewpan bring to a boil half a pound of "ghee" or butter, in which fry a finely shred onion to a crisp brown. Remove the onion, but *not* the butter, and into which last put a small handful of allspice, frying briskly for a minute; then add the rice, keeping it stirred till the grain turns colour. Now pour in some previously prepared stock, sufficient to more than immerse the rice; stir in a little salt, cover, and boil gently. As the liquid evaporates, uncover and stir constantly till the rice is cooked. Now let it steam by the fireside for ten minutes, stirring frequently, till the grains separate, when serve; garnishing with hard boiled eggs, your crisped onions, and some lightly fried raisins and sliced almonds.

SAVOURY DISHES.

"**Ballachow.**"—Wash, head, tail, and shell a pound of *small* sized prawns (if possible, not larger than those we get out yonder), and pound or grind them to a paste. Take six dry chillies or capsicums, a tablespoonful of salt, one whole garlic, two ounces of green ginger, and a pint of tamarind water. Mix these ingredients with half a pound of butter; add the prawn paste, and amalgamate the whole mass. Keep in glass bottles. When required for use, fry the paste with chopped onion and a little lemon peel. To be eaten as a zest with curry, or with bread and butter.

Indian Ramakin Toast.—Any kind of grated cheese, butter, and flour in equal quantities; measure with a tablespoon, and, for each spoonful of the ingredients, add the yolk of an egg; mix the whole well together, spread thickly on toast; brown in the oven, and serve hot. A sprinkling of cayenne pepper, mustard, pepper, and salt is an improvement.

Indian Mutton Cutlets.—Most old Indians, will, I think, admit that the cutlets out yonder are far superior to the home production ; so I give the following recipe, which I always find successful, not only with mutton, but with beef and chicken. In a machine, mince a pound of lean meat; mix with a finely chopped onion, a tablespoonful of chopped sweet herbs, and a little pepper and salt. Then mix in the yolks of two eggs; shape into flat discs, about three-quarters of an inch thick; dip each first into egg, then into breadcrumbs (on one side only), and fry till brown, turning occasionally.

Baked " Brinjal " Cutlets.—Prepare a pound of minced meat as if for above cutlets. Take six good sized "Brinjals" or egg vegetables, and boil them in salt and water. Divide them evenly—stalks and all—with a sharp knife; carefully scoop out the inside, which mix with your meat, and fry together for five minutes. Now refill the "Brinjals" with the mixture; dust with flour, and either bake in a slow oven or fry in " ghee " or butter. Green chillies or capsicums, finely chopped, may be added to taste.

"Dhobie," or Washerman Pie.—I am not prepared to state why this dish is so named, but I know it to be a favourite with us out there, especially where there are "young mouths" to fill. Cut your mutton—say two pounds—into convenient pieces; dust with pepper and salt, and *partially* broil the meat in a frying-pan. Now transfer it to a stewpan, pour on a little water, and let it simmer gently for about twenty minutes. Mash some potatoes—sufficient for the pie-dish you propose using— line the dish with the mash; put in your meat and gravy; add two tablespoonfuls of any sauce or ketchup; fit on a potato crust, paint over with yolk of egg, and bake in a slow oven for half an hour. An onion, sliced, is approved

of by some.   NOTE.—In making your potato crust, mix in
a little flour to give consistency and prevent sticking.

"Poofadh" or "Buffadh."—A dish peculiar to the
Eurasians, or Indo-Britons, but one by no means to be
despised.   Kill, clean, and truss a duck.   Get a capacious
stewpan; put in a cabbage, divided into four, then the
duck, entire.   Mix a little saffron powder in a large cup
of water and pour over the contents of the pan.   Now add
two onions, a tablespoonful of "ghee" or butter, a little
sliced green ginger, three green chillies or capsicums, half
a clove of garlic.   Cover and let simmer for an hour;
then uncover and let it go on simmering till done, but
taking care that the duck is not boiled to "rags."   Shortly
before serving, add two tablespoonsful of tamarind water,
vinegar, or lemon juice.

Chillie-Fry or "Vuddays."—Make a batter of two eggs
and a teaspoonful of self-raising flour.   Chop fine two
spring onions—stalks and all—two green chillies or capsicums, and a little salt and pepper.   Mix in the batter and
pour—a tablespoonful at a time—the mixture into a
frying-pan of "frizzling" butter.   As each cake is done
brown, take it out with a broad knife, and pour in more
batter, sufficient for another, and so on, till the whole
is finished.   Very nice eaten alone, or as a zest with
curry, &c.

Goanese "Tasta."—To be had in perfection in the
Bombay Presidency, when your cook is a native Portuguese.
Froth the whites of three eggs till the mass "stands"
of itself.   Take a small-sized frying-pan, and in it bring

two tablespoonsful of butter to the boil. Put in enough of the previously prepared white of egg till it occupies the whole area of the pan; place on a slow fire, and, when "set," drop in the yolks of the eggs, doing this *very* gently, so that they do not sink or break. Allow a little of the butter to run over the yolks to cook them. Garnish with fried sweet herbs, and serve hot.

"**Ding Dong.**"—Reduce to a paste four red chillies, a small piece of saffron, and half a garlic. Cut a pound of fat beef into thin slices, and rub into the meat a table-spoonful of moist sugar; then smear it with the paste, sprinkle with salt, and let it be for twelve hours. Thus prepared, the meat will keep for some time. When required, fry in a little "ghee" or butter, and eat with curry, or bread and butter.

"**Foogard.**"—Shell, head, and tail a dozen prawns (*i.e.*, according to size). Take a cabbage and steep it in salt water for half an hour, after which, drain and shred it finely; then place it in a saucepan, sprinkle with salt, and steam for a few minutes, or until the cabbage is parboiled. Now drain it. In a frying-pan heat a tablespoonful of "ghee" or butter; throw in some onion, sliced, two green chillies or capsicums, and four cloves of garlic, chopped fine; also the prawns. Fry the whole together for some minutes, stirring often. Now add your cabbage; mix it well with the other ingredients, pour in the milk of a whole cocoanut, previously extracted; give one boil, and serve with rice.

PUDDINGS, &C.

"**Bombay**" **Pudding.**—This is a misnomer; for, strangely enough, during our stay in the Bombay Presidency, we never had a cook who understood the making of this dish. Make a good sweet milk and egg custard, and in it soak some moderately thick slices of stale bread, and fry in "ghee" or butter to a light brown. Make a syrup of lemon juice and sugar; serve with the "fry," grating a little nutmeg and sifting a little white sugar over the whole.

Cocoanut Pudding.—In a pie-dish mix half a pound of grated cocoanut; the same weight of white sifted sugar; two tablespoonfuls of fresh butter; the whites of three or four eggs, whisked; a tablespoonful of brandy, and a teaspoonful of either orange or rosewater. Bake in a moderate oven.

Plantain or Banana Pudding.—In hot ashes roast a dozen of the fruit in their skins; then peel and cut them in slices; add sugar to taste; half a wine-glass of lemon juice, a little lemon peel finely chopped, a glass of sherry, a few cloves, and a lump of butter. Confine this in ordinary pudding paste and boil. To be served with cream.

Plantain or Banana "Poorrties" or Fritters.—Take half a dozen *ripe* fruit, cut them down the centre, fry till brown in "ghee" or butter, and sift with white sugar. The plantains must be very ripe, otherwise the astringent acridity of the fruit will render the dish uneatable.

Another Method.—Mash a dozen ripe fruit. Make a sweet custard of milk and eggs; mix it with the mash; gradually add a teaspoonful of flour; sweetening to taste; grate in a little nutmeg, and fry a tablespoonful of the mixture at a time in boiling butter. When nicely brown, sift on a little sugar, and serve hot.

"Raggi" Pudding.—In these days I have no doubt that "Raggi" is procurable in London; but under what name I regret my inability to say. Grind half a pound of the grain to flour, and have ready the following:—A pint of milk, two tablespoonfuls of sugar, the same quantity of butter, a whole cocoanut, quarter of a pound of almonds, ditto of raisins, a little salt. Make a breakfast cupful of cocoanut milk; mince the almonds very fine; set the milk on the fire, and, having mixed the sugar and "raggi" flour with the cocoanut milk, add it to the cow's milk as soon as it boils, stirring briskly. Give it another boil, and, when done, mix in the butter, almonds, and raisins. Pour into a dish previously buttered, and bake till brown.

Rice Pudding without Eggs.—Butter a dish and place in it a teacupful of fine washed rice. Fill the dish with cow's milk, add sugar to taste; put a lump of butter and grate a little nutmeg on the top; and bake till brown in a moderate oven.

SWEETS, &c.

"**Kulla-Kulla.**"—Take half a cocoanut, a breakfast cupful of butter, half a pound of moist sugar, three pounds of rice flour, three eggs, and a little salt. Extract half a breakfast cup of cocoanut milk; whisk the eggs—yolks separate from the whites; mix the eggs, flour, and salt with half the butter, adding cocoanut milk just sufficient to make the mass into dough. Now shape the dough into portions the size of small gingernuts, placing them gently on a well floured board, the compound being starchy and glutinous. Br ng to a boil the remainder of the butter, and fry several of the kulla-kullas at a time, till of a light brown; on removing, dust on some white sugar, and so on till all are done.

"**Komalunga.**"—Take a pound of sugar, and boil it to a thick syrup. Grate a pound of pumpkin, or vegetable marrow. Mix both together, and simmer over a gentle fire till the moisture disappears and the " confection " begins to show the sugar; pour in a few drops of any flavouring essence and lemon juice to taste; set out in flat dishes, previously buttered. If done well, it will be of the consistency of good Turkish Delight, and not stick to the knife when being cut.

Cocoanut Tablets.—Extract the milk from two cocoanuts, and boil it to a syrup with two pounds of moist
sugar: Scrape two more cocoanuts, which add to the
syrup ; also a pound of " kussa-kussa," or poppy-seed.
Keep on a slow fire, till you find the mixture harden on
being dropped in water. Butter a shallow tin, pour into
it, and, before it cools, divide it off into squares with a
knife.

" **Ulva** " or " **Hulwa.**"—Take a pound of " soojee," or
semolina, and, with a little water, work it well, and set it
by for the night. In the morning pour a little warm
water on the mass, mash thoroughly with a strong wooden
spoon, strain through a coarse cloth, and let the milk-like
liquid thus extracted stand for half the day. Now, with a
spoon, carefully remove any clear water you may find
standing on the surface of the extract. Have ready a
teacupful of almond paste (make it yourself), two pounds
of sugar, one pound of " ghee " or butter, and a phial of
strong rose water (*not* " utthur " of roses). Melt the
butter in a stewpan, pour in the " soojee " or semolina
extract, keep it on a gentle fire, and stir constantly for five
minutes. Now add the sugar, and continue boiling and
stirring for another five minutes, when put in the almond
paste, and go on boiling till the mass becomes translucent,
assaying frequently, until you find that a small portion of
the mixture, cooled on a plate, does not adhere to the
knife when cut, this being a sign that it is done. When
about half cooked, add the rose water to taste. (Some
people prefer a few drops of rose essence, obtainable at
the chemist.) Pour into small saucers, well buttered, and,
when cool, wrap in tissue paper, keeping in a dry place.

"**Dola-Dola**."—Make a thick syrup of a pound of sugar, and mix it with a pound of Bengal rice powder. Give it a gentle boil, after which add half a pound of sliced almonds, the milk of two cocoanuts, and a pint of melted butter. Boil all together till drops of the mixture harden in water, when pour into flat dishes.

Mango Fool.—The green fruit, I believe, is procurable at Whiteley's. Peel, stone, and shred a dozen green mangoes. Boil in water sufficient to cover, till the fruit is quite soft. Mash with a wooden spoon, and pass through a coarse sieve (the wires of which should be silvered). Sweeten to taste, and add any quantity of fresh milk, pouring it gradually and stirring briskly. Serve in custard glasses, topping each with grated nutmeg.

Flummery of Rice Flour.—To a teacupful of the flour add nearly a quart of fresh milk, sugar to taste, and a little lemon peel. Mix all smoothly together, avoiding lumps; boil until it thickens, when pour it into a blanc-mange or jelly mould, and turn out when quite cold, pouring over it some thick cream or sweet custard.

FRESH "SUMBALOOS" OR CHUTNIES.

These are made for any meal, where there is curry and rice. To obtain most of them to perfection, the grindstone and roller of the Indian menâge are *sine quâ non*. Get them from a stone-mason, made according to your directions, taking care the stone is not of a friable or floury consistency. Necessity has no law, and you will find, with a little practice, that you or your cook will be able to handle the "curry stone" as deftly as the "Thuonikurchi," or cook boy you have left behind you. I often sigh for either, or both. However, we can't get everything in this world, can we? The curry-stone once established, and its use mastered, you will find it invaluable in the practical working out of almost every recipe given in this little book.

Putcha "Poolsoo," or Brinjal "Sumbaloo."—Take two medium sized brinjals, or egg vegetables, roast them in hot ashes, skin and seed them. In a little "ghee" or butter fry a teaspoonful each of cummin and mustard seed, and half a garlic, reducing all three to a paste. In half a teacupful of *thick* tamarind water mix two red chillies, finely chopped; add the Brinjal pulp and the paste. Mix well together, and serve with the curry and rice.

Tomato or Love Apple "Sumbaloo."—Plunge two large tomatoes into boiling water. Take them out, peel them, and mash with a little salt. Slice thin two green chillies or capsicums, one onion, and chop up a little lemon peel. Mix all well together, squeeze in the juice of a lemon or add a tablespoonful of vinegar, and serve with curry and rice.

Shrimp "Sumbaloo."—Boil two dozen shrimps (more or less, according to size, if prawns), head, tail, and shell them; cut up into three or four, and mix with a little salt; add an onion finely chopped up, two green chillies similarly treated, a teacupful of cocoanut milk, a tablespoonful of lemon juice. Mix well together, and serve with any but meat curry, and rice.

Mango "Sumbaloo."—Mince up a half ripe mango very finely, one onion, and two green chillies or capsicums; add a little salt, half a teaspoonful of moist sugar, half a wine-glassful of tamarind water, vinegar, or lemon juice, and a teacupful of thick cocoanut milk. Mix all together, and serve with curry and rice.

Mint Chutney.—Take half-a-dozen sprigs of fresh mint, half an onion, half a garlic, two green or dry chillies or capsicums, an eggspoonful of salt, and a wineglassful of thick tamarind water. Grind all to a paste, and serve with curry and rice.

Cocoanut Chutney. — This is an universal favourite throughout India, and, if made well, is delicious. Take half a small sized cocoanut, rasp or pare off the inner

rind, and soak in boiling water; then crush it on the
curry stone; add a teaspoonful (more or less according to
palate) of cayenne pepper, salt, half a small onion, a few
cloves of garlic, and the squeeze of a lemon. Grind all
together to a paste, and serve with curry and rice.

"**Dhall,**" **or Split Lentils Chutney.**—Having sifted a
small cup of the grain free of impurities, dry it in a pan
over a little fire, and then pound it in a mortar to a
powder, or flour; convert it to a dough by mixing it with
a little weak tamarind water; add salt, a little cayenne
pepper, and half a garlic. Grind all together, and serve
with curry and rice, or Mulligatawny soup.

Tomato Chutney.—Plunge four ripe tomatoes into boiling
water; keep them there till soft. Then remove the skin
and seeds. To the pulp thus left add a teaspoonful of
vinegar or lemon juice, an eggspoonful of sugar, ditto of
salt, two chillies or capsicums, and half an onion finely
minced. Mix well, and serve with curry and rice.

BOTTLED CHUTNIES.

You can procure these ready-made in many varieties, but unless coming from friends, or *European* houses of business such as Spencers, or Oakes of Madras, and others in Bombay and Calcutta, they are rarely to be relied on. Our Aryan brothers are under the influence of the spirit of the age, equally with the dishonest English tradesman, and the tendency to adulterate is as strong out there as it is here. Given, then, that the ingredients are procurable, and an Oriental " connection " is wanting, the subjoined recipes will, I hope, prove useful.

Tomato Chutney.—Select a dozen fine ripe tomatoes, scald them in boiling water, take off the skin, and seed them. Set aside the pulp, and squeeze all the *débris* through a coarse cloth. Now boil the pulp in the juice till thick, when add a tablespoonful of salt, ditto of moist sugar, and the following, finely chopped :—one garlic, six green or red chillies or capsicums, two medium-sized green ginger roots. Continue boiling till the mass becomes quite stiff, using a slow fire, and stirring assiduously with a wooden spoon. Now take another utensil; in it melt a teacupful of " ghee " or butter, and fry a sliced onion ; when well fried, add the contents of the other pan, and go on simmering and stirring occasionally. As soon as the grease rises to the surface, you will know it is done. Cool and fill into chutney bottles or jars. Some add vinegar or lemon juice.

Sweet Lime, or Lucknow Chutney.—Take one dozen limes, or in their stead half a dozen fresh lemons; cut up the fruit into small pieces; mix with half a pound of salt, and place in the sun for half a day. Take a quarter pound of green ginger and a quarter pound of garlic, half a pound each of stoned plums, currants, almonds, and dry dates. Chop all rather fine, and mix with one pound of chillie powder. In a quart of vinegar boil the limes or lemons, and when the fruit turns brown add all the other ingredients, bottling when cold.

Dry Fruit Chutney.—Take a quarter pound of garlic, half a pound each of currants, dried apricots, dates, dried chillies, moist sugar, and dry ginger; one pound each stoned raisins, almonds, and figs, one tablespoonful of salt, and a tablespoonful of powdered allspice. Place all in a soup tureen, or other large vessel (crockery), pour on vinegar sufficient to moisten the whole mass; allow it to soak for a whole day, after which grind to a paste, and put away in bottles or jars.

Sweet Bengal Chutney. — Take the following ingredients : quarter pound each of raisins, currants, chillies, and garlic, half a pound of almonds and dates, two tablespoonfuls of moist sugar, a root of ginger, one dessertspoonful of salt. Grind all to a smooth paste, mix

in a bottle of vinegar, and put away in chutney bottles or
jars.

Kashmere Chutney.—Grind to a paste the following :—
quarter pound each of mustard seed, stoned raisins,
chillies, and salt ; half a pound each of green ginger and
garlic. Dissolve one pound of moist sugar in two quarts
of vinegar; mix with the paste; bottle and use after
having been kept in the sun for three weeks,

PICKLES.

Indian Onion Pickle.—Take two pounds of small white onions (the size of cherries), strip off the outer skins, and put into a wide-mouthed jar with two tablespoonfuls of salt; place in the sun for a week, daily removing any water that may be secreted. Now add an ounce of sliced green ginger, two whole garlics, two tablespoonfuls of moist sugar, and fill up with vinegar. Again place out in the sun, when you will find the onions to eat short and crisp, and be far preferable to the English-made article.

Lime or Lemon Pickle.—Take two dozen limes or one dozen lemons; cut in four, but not quite through; introduce salt into the cuts, place on a flat dish, and set out in the sun for ten days. In an enamelled pan mix a tablespoonful of mustard seed, ditto of cummin seed, a quart of salad oil, and a quart of vinegar. Then throw in the fruit, two tablespoonfuls of sugar and chillie powder to taste. Stir and boil till the fruit is tender, and bottle when cool.

Mango Pickle in Oil.—Take a dozen green mangoes, free of "string" and turpentine. Peel, stone, and cut in four. Place on a flat dish, plentifully sprinkle with salt, and set in the sun for ten days. (Note :—Wipe your knife after each cut, otherwise the fruit will turn black.) Then bruise a tablespoonful of cummin and mustard seed mixed. Pour a quart of salad oil into an enamel saucepan, add the seed, and give it a boil. Now add an eggspoonful of chillie powder ; then pour in a quart and a half of vinegar, three tablespoonfuls of sugar ; take the pan off the fire, and throw in the mangoes. Let it stand till cool, when bottle. The older this pickle is the better.

MISCELLANEOUS.

Chief Requirements for Indian Cookery. Implements, &c.—The grindstone and roller; a mincing and sausage machine; a cocoanut scraper (any working ironmonger can make it under your directions); several wooden spoons of sizes; an "iyappah," or basket work lid to your "rice pot," for drawing the "cunjee" water (to be made to order by a basket weaver); a kitchen clock; a slate, suspended at a convenient height by the clock, with a slate pencil secured with twine, to chalk up the "times" necessary for the different processes; a mill.

Ingredients, &c.—Curry powder; curry paste; tamarind in any form but unsweetened; cocoanuts; dry chillies; green chillies or capsicums; "ghee," butter, lard, or dripping; limes or lemons; rice of sorts; green ginger; dry ginger; a well-filled spice box; "dhall" or split lentils; saffron; mustard, coriander, and cummin seeds; onions; garlic.

Attributes.—Patience and a sunny temper, both on the part of yourself and cook.

How to Make Madras Curry Paste.—Take one pound coriander seed, quarter pound saffron, quarter pound dry chillies, half a pound black pepper, quarter pound mustard seed, two ounces dry ginger, two ounces " vendium," two ounces garlic, half pound salt, half pound sugar, two ounces cummin seed, half a pound dried pea flour, half a pound cardamon and cinnamon mixed. Clean, dry, pound, and sift the whole; place in a large pan, and while over a slow fire mix in as much salad oil and vinegar by alternate wineglassesful as will convert the mixture to a stiffish paste, when bottle and cork well. This paste is used chiefly for mulligatawny soup, but it makes delicious curries as well.

How to Make Madras Curry Powder.—Take three pounds coriander seed, three-quarter pound saffron, three-quarter pound dry chillies, three-quarter pound pepper, three-quarter pound mustard seed, six ounces dry ginger, four ounces " vendium," three-quarter pound salt, three-quarter pound sugar, six ounces cummin seed, quarter pound poppy seed, quarter pound mixed spices, one pound dried pea flour. Clean, dry, pound, and sift the whole, and keep in well-corked bottles.

How to Make Bombay Curry Powder.—Take three pounds coriander seed, half a pound cummin seed, one and half pound turmeric, four ounces fenugreek, half a pound mustard seed, one pound pepper, one and quarter pound dry chillies. Clean, dry, pound, and sift the whole, and keep in well-corked bottles.

How to Make Bengal Curry Powder.—Take three pounds coriander seed, three and half pounds turmeric, twelve ounces fenugreek, three pounds dry ginger, three pounds black pepper, two pounds dry chillies, one pound cinnamon, one pound cardamon. Clean, dry, pound, and sift the whole, and keep in well-corked bottles.

How to Make " Ghee."—Use a large pan. Take any quantity of butter (so long as it does not more than half fill the pan), place on a slow fire and boil. When it threatens to bubble over, sprinkle with cold water. After several boils, throw in a handful of bay or mint leaves ; give one more boil, allow to cool, and, before it congeals, pour it into wide-mouthed bottles or jars, cork down, and keep dry.

How to Make Tamarind Water.—Take, say, a teacupful of the dry or preserved fruit, put it into a bowl, and pour over it a large breakfast cupful of boiling water ; break up the tamarind with a wooden spoon, and allow it to soak for five minutes. Now with your fingers mash the fruit well, pass the mixture through a coarse cloth, and use the juice. This quantity is about enough for a family curry or mulligatawny. If you have the preserved tamarind, to avoid over sweetness wash away the syrup, and scrape the fruit a little before immersing it in the hot water.

How to Extract the Milk from a Cocoanut.—Break the nut —shell and all—into halves, and, with your scraper, scrape out the contents, stopping just short of the rind. Place the scrapings into a bowl, and pour on boiling water sufficient to cover the mass. After letting it stand for five minutes, work it well with your fingers, and, when the water assumes the appearance and consistency of rich milk, take up " fistfuls " of the scrapings, squeeze well, and put aside ; then strain the milk through a coarse cloth. If

E

you want it to be very rich let it stand for a couple of hours, when you will find the pure cocoanut milk at the top and the water beneath. Some make a second "brew," pouring more water over the recovered husk, but there is no strength in it, at least none to be appreciated.

How to Make Madras "Apums" or Hoppers.—I have never tried these in this country; an important ingredient, viz., fresh cocoanut "toddy,' being an impossibility. However, yeast, they say, is a good substitute, so with it the attempt may be made. Take, then, a pound of any rice, four cocoanuts, an ounce of white salt, and a teacupful of yeast, which, I presume, is stronger in its action than "toddy." Reduce the rice, half to very fine and the other half to coarse flour; put this last in a pan, pour two teacups of hot water, and set aside for ten minutes; then stir in the fine rice flour, half the yeast, and the salt; sprinkle a little wheaten flour on the top. Having done all this in the evening, cover the pan containing the mixture and set by for the night. Early in the morning milk the four cocoanuts, stir into the mixture, and pour half a teacupful at a time on a flat pan containing a little butter, and standing on a clear but low fire; cover the pan with another one containing hot embers, and let cook for three minutes. The above quantities should make a dozen cakes.

How to Make Madras "Apums" or Hoppers. (Another Way.)—These cakes make such delicious eating, especially for "chota hazri," or early breakfast, that I am induced to give another recipe, which, however, is not mine. "Wash and clean a pound of rice very nicely, and lay it upon a cloth in the sun; when quite dry pound it to a fine flour; then put it in a pan and mix it to a paste with sweet ' toddy ' or yeast, letting it remain for at least twelve hours, or all the night. Next morning take two cocoanuts, scrape the ins des, and squeeze the juice into the rice paste, mixing well; then place an iron or earthen pan on a rather slow fire, rub the inside of the pan with " ghee " or butter, and put as much as you please of the mixture in it; cover it over with a similar pan, and place some embers on the top. In a short while it will be baked, which can only be known by lifting the top; if not done enough let it remain a little longer, but do not turn it. To make the variety called Egg Hoppers, the yolks of three eggs and a tablespoonful of moist sugar, mixed with the " toddy," or yeast, is added to the rice flour. This makes the cakes yellow and sweet. The addition of a few cake seeds sprinkled over each, as it cooks, is an improvement.

How to Make " Chupaties."—Mix flour (wheaten) and water with a little salt into a stiff dough, kneading it well. Butter or " ghee " may be added to taste. Milk, too, may be substituted for water. Roll the dough very thin, or flatten it out with the hands, and smear on both sides with " ghee " or butter, and bake in a flat pan on a moderate fire. These cakes form an agreeable change from rice with curry.